THE LIFE CYCLE OF A

CHICKEN

By Robin Merritt

Published by The Child's World®
1980 Lookout Drive
Mankato, MN 56003-1705
800-599-READ
www.childsworld.com

The Child's World®: Mary Berendes, Publishing Director
The Design Lab: Kathleen Petelinsek, design
Red Line Editorial: Editorial direction

Photographs ©: Shutterstock Images, cover (top left, bottom left, bottom right), 1 (top left, bottom left, bottom right), 3, 9, 22, 26, 30 (top); Saied Shahin Kia/iStockphoto, cover (top right), 1 (top right), 10, 31 (bottom); Jean Frooms/iStockphoto, 5; iStockphoto, 6; Saied Shahin Kiya/Shutterstock Images, 13; Magdalena Jankowska/iStockphoto, 14, 31 (middle); Yuriy Poznukhov/iStockphoto, 17; David Kay/Shutterstock Images, 18, 31 (top); Daniel Cardiff/iStockphoto, 21; Abraham Badenhorst/iStockphoto, 25, 30 (bottom); Borko Ćirić/iStockphoto, 29

ISBN: 978-1-60973-144-1
LCCN: 2011927700

Printed in the United States of America
Mankato, MN
July 2011
PA02089

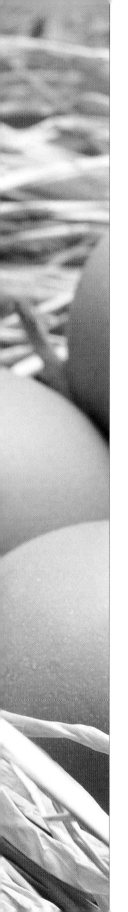

TABLE OF

CONTENTS

LIFE CYCLES

Every living thing has a life cycle. A life cycle is the steps a living thing goes through as it grows and changes. Humans have a life cycle. Animals have a life cycle. Plants have a life cycle, too.

A cycle is something that happens over and over again. A life cycle begins with the start of a new life. It continues as a plant or creature grows. And it keeps going as one living thing creates another, or **reproduces**— and the cycle starts over again.

A chicken's life cycle has three main steps: egg, chick, and adult chicken.

Chickens and flowers have life cycles.

Chickens can be many sizes and colors.

CHICKENS

Chickens are medium-sized birds. All birds have feathers and wings, but not all birds can fly. Birds eat with their beaks. Female birds lay eggs.

Chickens are one of the most common birds in the world. Chickens can live to be about ten years old.

Most farm chickens are raised for their eggs and meat. Family farm chickens sleep in a chicken coop. This keeps them safe from **predators**, such as foxes. Chickens can fly, but they cannot fly very far. They can only fly far enough to perch on a fence or get away from danger.

A baby chicken is a chick. How does it fit into the life cycle of a chicken?

A small, yellow chick feels soft and fits perfectly in your hand.

A chick uses its egg tooth when it is ready to **hatch**.

HATCHING

The life cycle begins inside an egg. The baby bird inside grows an egg tooth. This is a small, sharp piece on its beak. When the chick is ready to hatch, it uses its egg tooth to crack the shell of the egg. First, a small hole appears in one end of the egg. The chick keeps pecking until the end of the shell breaks off. This can take a whole day.

CHICK

Once the egg is broken, the chick slowly crawls out. The chick is wet and weak. It stays close to its mother to rest and keep warm. After a few hours, the chick is dry. A newborn can see, walk, eat, and drink.

A chick has down feathers. They are soft and fluffy. These feathers keep the chick warm as it grows.

As the baby bird grows inside the egg, the chick has to bend to fit.

Chicks peck the ground to find food.

Like its mother, the chick pecks the ground looking for seeds, insects, and worms to eat. The mother hen scratches the grass to help her young find food. After a few weeks, the chicks can find food without her help.

In a field, a chick can lose sight of its mother in the tall grass. The chick chirps so its mother can find it. The mother clucks to call her chick. Even in a farmyard, chicks still chirp a lot so their mothers can find them. The chicks can be very loud.

Chicks stay close to their mother after hatching.

The comb and wattle of a chicken are often red.

GROWING

The chick grows quickly. The egg tooth falls off after a few days. Within a few weeks, the chick starts to grow adult feathers. Adult birds have two layers of feathers: tough outer feathers and soft down next to their skin. A fleshy crest called a comb starts to grow on the top of the chick's head. A fleshy flap of skin called a wattle grows under its beak.

In six months, the chick is a full-grown chicken. A male is called a rooster. A female is called a hen. Chickens live in a group called a flock. The roosters in a flock watch out for danger. A rooster is usually larger and more colorful than a hen. Roosters have longer tail feathers and larger combs on their heads. Roosters are louder than hens, too. Hens can only cluck.

A rooster's "cock-a-doodle-doo" can wake a whole farm.

Many hens lay eggs with brown shells.

HENS LAY EGGS

When a hen is six months old, she is ready to lay eggs. A hen can lay more than 200 eggs a year. But not all of these eggs become chicks. Only eggs that have been **fertilized** when a hen mates with a rooster can become chicks. Many eggs are not fertilized. They do not become chicks. Instead, these eggs are sold as food for people to eat.

The hens take care of the eggs. Some hens even lay eggs together in the same nest. They lay their eggs in a nest of straw in the chicken coop. A hen lays an egg almost every day until there are about 12 eggs in the nest. This is called a **clutch**. Then she **incubates**, or sits on the eggs to keep them warm. The hen's warmth helps the chicks grow inside the eggs.

When a hen incubates, her body covers the eggs.

An **embryo** begins to form on the egg yolk.

INSIDE AN EGG

An embryo, or unborn chick, grows inside each egg. The embryo starts as a small spot on the egg yolk. The embryo gets food from the yellow yolk. The egg white around the yolk is like a cushion for the embryo and yolk. The embryo grows larger and looks more and more like a chick. The egg's shell protects the growing chick inside the egg.

After about 21 days, the unborn chick has grown to fill the shell. The hen can hear her chick peeping inside the egg. She clucks back to it. The chick is ready to hatch, and the life cycle of a chicken continues.

Chicks hatch and continue their lives outside the egg.

LIFE CYCLE DIAGRAM

Egg in Nest

Hen Incubating

Adult Chicken

Chick

Chick Hatching

Web Sites

Visit our Web site for links about the life cycle of a chicken: **childsworld.com/links**

Note to Parents, Teachers, and Librarians: We routinely verify our Web links to make sure they are safe and active sites. So encourage your readers to check them out!

Books

Martin, Claudia. *Farming*. New York, NY: Marshall Cavendish Benchmark, 2010.

Miller, Sara Swan. *Chickens*. New York, NY: Children's Press, 2000.

Ross, Michael Elsohn. *Life Cycles*. Brookfield, CT: Millbrook Press, 2001.

Glossary

clutch (KLUCH): A clutch is a batch of eggs. A hen lays a clutch.

embryo (EM-bree-oh): An embryo is an organism in the early stages of growth. A chick starts out as an embryo.

fertilized (FUR-tuh-lyzd): Fertilized refers to an egg that can grow and develop into a new life. A chicken egg that is fertilized can become a chicken.

hatch (HACH): To hatch is to break out of an egg. Chicks hatch after about 21 days in their eggs.

incubates (ING-kyuh-bayts): When an animal incubates, it keeps eggs warm before they hatch. A hen incubates by sitting on her eggs.

predators (PRED-uh-turs): Predators are animals that hunt and eat other animals. Sleeping in coops helps chickens stay safe from predators.

reproduces (ree-pruh-DOOS-ez): If an animal or plant reproduces, it produces offspring. A chicken pair reproduces and creates new chicks.

Index